Becoming the Sea

poems

Immanuel Suttner

Merchavaya Publishing
PO Box 1753
Bondi Junction, NSW, 1355
In association with *Quartz Press*
13 Connaught Towers, 15 Kent Road
Dunkeld West, 2196, Johannesburg

First edition published 5785 (2025)
Typeset by Porat Jacobson
Cover Design by Porat Jacobson
Cover photograph by Shirley Brockwell
Printed and bound by mixam.com.au
ISBN: 978-0-9584023-0-9

These poems were written over several
years and some of them have appeared
online or in print. Acknowledgement is
due to the editors of publications such
as Quadrant. Prosopisia, Voices Israel
Group of Poets in English, and ARC
30 (IAWE - The Israel Association of
Writers in English).

*To the life and legacy of Zvi and Batya
Jaspan, and all their descendants, to the
life force that took the shape of Ella, my
beautiful guardian and companion in a
dog suit, to Shirley Eisenberg Brockwell
who mends, creates and builds, to my late
father Ron Suttner and my late mother
Freda Toker-Suttner, and to Marcia
Leveson, who remained a friend.*

perhaps
like me
when you were small
you stood, before some childhood game,
as teams were picked
your heart anxiously
shouting inside
choose me, choose me
longing for that validation
that proof you were acceptable
if so
now is the time
to bend over
and calmly and firmly
tell that child:
you are already chosen

once I knew a man
who turned into a sparrow
out of sheer embarrassment
he hid his bowler hat
and umbrella
behind his smile
and flew sheepishly out the window
have you seen that man?
if so, tell him, I beseech you,
that I love him
that the world was not made only
for the brutal and the brute
tell him
if he will fly back to me
I will hold him
while he
chirps

friday night
in a brand new sterile hotel
next to a rugby stadium in cronulla
where people mostly
drink to forget

no one here
in a thousand
years
has heard of
covering the challah
so it won't be embarrassed
when the wine gets blessed first,
to sanctify the day
on which doing
returned to being.

I don't know, if just
passing through, I could
satisfactorily
explain it. but anyway
no one is asking

I go up to my room,
furnished with instantly
forgettable things,
and quietly welcome
the sabbath queen

Shuffle

shuffle starts off
rather slow
the limbs must learn
to feel the flow

then we shuffle
running man
there seems no end
to what we can

we spin and t-step
side to side
the body and the
one inside

then we shuffle
to the chair
the walker and the
blanket there

the dance, the dance
open and close
the heart it watches, feels
and knows

Good Neighbours

the little dog
next door died
apparently
in his sleep
curled up
in his bed

I'd never seen him
only heard his
pleasant yap
when his owner
returned
from her 12 hour
lollipop shifts

or when my dog Ella and he
chatted through the fence
her basso profundo
and his small man bark

and now there is silence
and tho I never knew him
I miss him

my friend had a dream
in which we were
joined at café zigolinis,
by her dead-at-ninety father,
as dapper as ever,
dressed in a pristine
blue suit and tie
his skin unblemished
(she'd last seen him withered)

and after we had sat a while
he bounced up,
announced he was going home
brushed away her offer of assistance,
and walked off with a spring in his step
for death had taken years off his life.

Hidden Treasure

I look at
the sadness
in my
chest
it is like
a rectangular
box
muted in
colour
somewhat
heavy
taking
up a
lot of space
so there is
hardly room
for anything else
I open it
inside it
surprisingly
are long car trips
beach sand and
dog hairs
starfish and stars
children playing
'till night fall
and old men
sipping tea and laughing

last night
I went to the *shavuot service*
at the little *shul*
down the road
which struggles
to keep going
its members
mostly over seventy
their children
far away
or not so interested

and after the communal dinner
with seventeen people
on a chilly winter night
everyone went home
except for me and a friend
leaving the young
recently hired rabbi,
who had prepared a
shtikel toira
to learn and teach
as is the custom
on this harvest festival
of receiving the torah,
without much of
a congregation

so we stayed back
not wanting him to be alone
and took turns reading
what he had prepared
about whether the torah
was a gift or a purchase

and how *moshe* our teacher
persuaded the angels
to let it come down
to this world below

and although I did not
fully resonate
with the details, or feel they
described my being's
deepest longings, still we
generated some warmth
and the kindness was real

so
closing my eyes
I basked in the light

it took me
more than
an hour
to hang up
the washing
with many
pauses
for contemplation

the wonder
of a crumbling
clothes peg
the perfect
wrinkles
in a fitted sheet
the flies
on a turd
literally turning
shit
into Life

watching the clothes line
dancing in the wind
I don't know
which is more
beautiful
the foreground
the background
or the
pure liquid
knowing

loneliness taught me how to be lonely
cleverness how to be smart
but wisdom sailed right over my head
and settled some distance apart

misery taught me misery
pleasure taught how to moan
I stood on the hilltop and
looked for a friend
somebody that I could call home

somebody that I could call home
across the miles and years
they with me and I with them
beneath the laughter and tears

Advice for Grieving

when loss comes
as it will
and you tell yourself
you are drowning
in a dull ache
or a sharp pain
hold on
hold on to this
as your life raft

not onto platitudes
not onto imaginary
better futures
but on to
the familiar air
coming into your nostrils
the rise of your chest
the movement in your abdomen

hold on to
the pain
sharp and crisp as burnished steel
a sword to petty concerns
a fire to singe vanities
bringing you closer
than you've ever been
to the heart of the mystery

like the morning
you rise early
to embark upon some
great journey

hold on
to those with you
at this birth
into a different life
that will reveal itself
as you go

when I was a young man
my father wanted to
place his hands on my head
and give me the blessing
jewish fathers give to their sons:
"eloheem yasimcha
ke'efrayim oo che'menashe...
may g-d make you
like efraim and like menasheh"

and I did not allow him
because I had formed
judgements about him
of the sort children,
in the fog of youth,
form of their parents

and now that he has been
in the grave
and in my heart
eleven years
and I am older
and understand
I say to him:

forgive me
forgive me
forgive me

and I say to myself
forgive me

Hero 1:01

I have a friend
who cannot sleep at night
he listens to music
or watches the dark
outline of trees. like sheep
his mistakes pass before him
and he numbers them one by one
but with dawn he somehow rises
and does what needs to be done

hanging a large sheet
over dining room chairs
because of the incessant rain

I crawl under the table
to spread the edges
and find myself
in a mystery world

four years old again

Poem for Ella on *Shavuot*

my dog was like ruth
where I went
she went
and my people were
her people
and 'tho she was desexed
by the animal rescue place
before we brought her home
perhaps the Self of all
that I am told is always present
and which knows no obstacle it cannot overcome

will establish for her
a *yad veshem*
and birth from her loins
the redemption

Obituary for a Dog *(Seder Klavim)*

the service of dog is now complete:
she barked her barks
smelt her odours
marked her posts with her urine
deposited her droppings
enjoyed the marrow of her bones
wagged her tail and licked
with her pink generous tongue

chased her cats
and accompanied her people
never lied
always faithful
with every sinew
and drop of saliva
to her dogness

therefore it is said:
the service of the dog is now complete
according to all its laws and regulations
and may her portion be
in the rebuilt and replanted
garden of eden
with a ball, and grass, a bird
and a bone
and one eye open
for the *shechina*
dressed in Her coat of many forms
who will arrive at the gate
and call her softly
to follow freely

roll and run
with new friends and old
in the fields of green

and I will be there
to glance back at, return to

both invisibly tethered
at the heart

Instructions for Living from the Dog

leave no smell
unsmelt
leave no tree
unanointed
leave no bird
unchased
leave no grass
unrolled in
leave no noise
unbarked at
no morsel
ungobbled
no friend
unlicked

often I fantasize
about a job
where I can be truthful
every minute of the day
and don't nod my head
because of fear of loss
at things that make no
sense to me
something like
pushing seedlings
into soft loamy soil
watering trees
talking to rocks
maybe
pushing a river
downstream

"They've Stolen My Lights"

some acquaintances of mine
took some of my lights
that blink on and off
like stars in the sky
and used them at a party
to which they did not
invite me
and so enraged and hurt was I
I temporarily forgot
they had left me
the moon
and the stars

On Being a Zio

you call me a 'zio'
as some kind of derogatory
pejorative label
like 'nigga', or 'commie', or 'faggot'
but I'm not just a zio, although
I stand in human solidarity with Israelis, as
contradictory and coffee-drinking a people as any
other.

I'm a vegetable growing zio
a concerned about the size of the electricity bill zio
a dog walking zio
a pick up litter at the beach zio
a singing in the shower zio
a dip in the sea zio
an argue with my children zio
a swear at drivers who don't let me in zio
a netflix bingeing zio
a vegan alternatives zio
a love-finding-common ground-with-my-fellow-
australians zio
a wanting to feel at home wherever I am zio
a take-comfort-in-chocolate when your malice and
blindness get all to much zio

Maya

I am texting on snapchat
with maya williams
ostensibly a young
and bodacious
australian woman
who has no problem
sharing with me
pictures of her
naked body in
hyper suggestive poses

but her odd
turns of phrase, incorrect case
and lack of verb-subject
agreement are easy clues
I am chatting with, in this case,
a west african male, one of
a vast army of scammers who,
like scavengers on a rubbish dump,
or destitute miners on gold tailings
trying to extract a microgram here or there,
forage the lonely bloated disconnected psyches of the
first world male, hoping to reel something big in with
'shaved pussy' and 'fuck buddy'
after which it's just a matter
of transferring a small deposit across and then she/he
will be mine, all mine, all mine

he dangles breasts I dangle dollars,
and we play along, quite willingly and happily, for a bit,
both clinging to our mirages
the conversation is hot and sweaty but punctuated with
'are you going to send the money now'
and at a certain point it pales,

and once lovers turn to bitter enemies as I call out the
scam with the impolite equivalents of
'pond scum' 'bottom feeder' 'canine faeces' et al, and
he replies
in less eloquent, grammatically incorrect second-
language-speaker insults before abruptly
disappearing back into that same ether from which

maya williams,
a short while prior,
had so mysteriously reached out to me
so young
so beautiful
so once full of promise

there is a little
one-back-from-the-corner
fruit-and-veg store
owned by an immigrant
chinese couple
that I walk to
three or four times a week
when I need a break
from the walls of my cave

and I always buy something small
to give the little guy
my money
instead of the retail giant
just down the road

a bag of tomatoes
a bunch of bananas
and we smile and greet each other
exchange a few pleasantries
and never get beyond that

I don't know their names
and they don't know mine
yet we are in a relationship

The Thread

the search party
for a person
trapped on the far
side
of a very deep and
steep crevasse
shot an arrow
across

and attached to the
arrow was a thread
and attached to the thread
was a string
and attached to the string
was a thin rope
and attached to the thin rope
was a heavy rope
and attached to the heavy rope
was a steel cable
and attached to the steel cable
was a lightweight bridge
which the person
who had been stuck
was able to pull over
and crawl across
to be reunited
with those they love

and the thread's name
is connection and hope

the way consumerism
grinds you down
with its special character
and one Capital passwords
with its
'laziness penalty'
premiocre products
insurance premium increases

with its debit orders
that drain,
your bank account
while you sleep,
with its
meaningless choices
inadequacy advertising
and sticky web
of 'buy now pay later'
that waters addiction
and lays you down
on astroturf

the way consumerism
grinds you down
with its trailing commissions
and hungry functionaries
power dressed
to hide transaction fees
with its scripted call centres
permanently experiencing
higher than usual
call volumes

the way consumerism
wears you down
with its spiralling complexity,

its facsimile of service,
its efficiency *shtik*
its worship of convenience
its pretence of consultation

with its funnelling customers
and marketing metrics
and mountains of junk
put out on the verge

with its tales told by idiots
"full of sound and fury
signifying nothing"

Tru Blu

our burgers
are made from australian cows
raised by australian farmers
who, after drinking australian spirits
drive over australian wombats
on their way back from the pub

our snags are made
with australian hands
and australian nervous systems
using australian soy and corn,
australian molecules and only
the finest
australian atoms
for australian conditions and
australian digestive systems.

our burgers
are made from australian cows
killed in australian slaughterhouses
by australian workers
born in 17 different countries
one of whom
in his tea break
checks his sports betting app
only to find
his australian horse, leg broken,
has been politely green-screened
and shot with an
australian bullet

Five Senses Dance

we come
into the space
a little cold
a little closed
each stiff with what burdens the heart
begin to move
open to the feelings
dance with our conditioning
dance with our sorrow
dance with our hips, our buttocks, our joy
dance with our autumn
and dance with our spring
some couple with others, appear playful and open
others more inward, eyes closed, dance alone
some utilise the space
some cling to a corner
everyone goes
on the journey for them
and as petals unfurl
and soften to the dance,
the evaluative mind
with its judgment and chatter
subsides into surcease
the beauty of each
unrepeatable form
shining through body
and face
is revealed

Tikun Chatzot (Geulah Zeirah)

once in jerusalem
very late
I took the no. 9 bus home
and on the way
at a flashing light
saw a road gang
fixing a pothole
that meant at least as much
as rebuilding the
beyt ha'mikdash

Zachor Ve'shamor

sometimes I pity the *charedi yidden*
with their *tsholent* bellies
and their fish bowl eyes
who never know a moments rest
cos' even on *shabbos*
they still have to
keep and
remember

as the light was fading
looking at the bay
and the big jet liners
coming into land

I stood there
saying
"please hashem
please hashem"

and I had no idea
what I was asking for

but the longing to see
what the world is hiding
felt too big for a
body to contain

Invisible Mending

tho' it's there in plain sight
most of her household does not yet see
how she loads the dishwasher
cleans the surfaces
clears the gutters
makes the crooked straight
spends years repairing
what others ruptured in weeks
listens, calms and validates
holds the line
stitches a family
or a friendship
at the fraying point
so that others
may wear their best lives

Birth

c'mon g-d
you're doing well
one more big push

and
yes

look

here comes
the universe

In Praise of Darkness

in light
potatoes turn green
skin burns

in darkness
seeds begin
their journey

in light
things
bend towards familiarity

in darkness
the familiar
requires investigation

in light
we are busy

in darkness
we slow

in light
it seems
we have figured it out
in darkness we are less

certain we know

the ground is pushing at my feet
the clouds weigh down on me
because wherever I may go
my thoughts accompany

if I can find that verdant isle
where thought was never seen
I'll gently lay my heavy head
upon its fields of green

I Wish You A Long Life

it takes seven years to recover
from the shock of being born
it takes seven years to recover from giving birth
it takes seven years to recover from school
it takes seven years to recover from work
It takes seven years to recover
from relocation and emigration
it takes seven years to recover
from the death of loved ones
it takes seven years to recover
from being made redundant
it takes seven years to recover from divorce
it takes seven years to recover
from the realisation more's behind than ahead
so may you live
long enough to recover

Comfort

when I imagine
being dead
it's not from an accident
or violent attack
its in peaceful
suburbia

the mourners have gathered
under the whispering trees
the rabbi says her thing
and I'm lying there
a bit claustrophobic
in my *tachrichim*
and perhaps my plain pine box

then I'm lowered into the hole
its dark
I hear the thud thud thud
as family and friends
kindly put three shovelfuls of earth
into my grave
and perhaps I experience a mild panic
"how am I going to get out of here?"
I'm dead
and yet in these fantasies
I'm still a perceiving knowing centre
so what, after all, has died?

if there's nothing after death,
then
there's nothing to be afraid of
and no one to be afraid of it

but if Awareness persists
beyond the setting of the body-mind
you only get one life
but that life is forever

either way
you can't lose

first there was just g-d
then there was me and g-d
then there was me, a wife, and g-d
then there was me, a wife, a family, and g-d
then there was me, a wife, a family, a dog, and g-d
then there was me, half a family, a dog, and g-d
then there was me, a dog, and g-d
then there was just me and g-d
then there was just g-d

Idyll

I am driving to shul
on yom kippur
and my parents,
both dead
these many years
and not always so happily married,
sit in the back seat
holding hands

Party (In Memoriam Alexi)

I am part of a transitional programme
which only lasts for a limited time
so today I had a farewell session
with a client who lived for years under a bridge,
has been smoking since 14, so unsurprisingly,
now in his seventies, has advanced chronic
obstructive pulmonary disease

a noisy grader, levelling a future bicycle path,
burped and bellowed a few metres beyond his fence
behind which we sat in the little courtyard
of his public housing unit
as the traffic flowed by

now safely homed, his cupboard full,
his schizophrenia well managed
he pulled out some beers and green olives,
a packet of cheese and onion chips, slices of
processed cheese, opened a tin of squashed sardines.
I ate the olives, drank the beer,
grimaced my way through the sardines
which although I ate them as a sacrificial offering
suddenly tasted good,
even had a slice of cheese out of respect
for his hospitality, soothing myself
with the thought the cow's male bobby calves were
already dead, beyond any suffering, perhaps the cow
also

he ate, because he had company, otherwise he has no
appetite, and is wasting away, as we sat and he plied
me with beers

and fished olives from the bottom of the jar,
and folded his cheese - once he was a sheet metal worker -
into neat cheese sandwiches

alcohol steaming lightly from my ears,
a spirit libation to the Most High,
he rolled himself a cigarette,
coughed and spluttered his way through it
and we had ourselves a picnic party

and around us
and between us
and through us
g-d flowed
in g-d's mysterious way

market forces
have got to
the honeysuckle
the jasmine
and the frangipani
please tap
or swipe here
to release
their scent

I say to the trees, straggling
between asphalt and the mall
rescue us please

I say to the milk cows
lowing for their stolen calves
rescue us please

I say to the shark
sinking finless in the depths
rescue us please

for we know not what we do

Running the City to Surf

the city to surf I ran alone
without a true friend
without a true home

plasticup shards
formed an angry sea
dark footprint of human
loomed over me
from the barbies
the ex cows asked
wistfully:

"what has all this to do with me?"

Confusion

I've been to the west and I've been to the east
and I'm bloated with spirit like a warm bowl of yeast
I've been to the ashram, I've been on retreat
I've sat in the silence, I've stopped eating meat

I'm so enlightened I can't find my head
perhaps it has rolled away under the bed
I've been to satsang and I've been such a whore
and yet I'm no settled than I was before

Psalm of Immanuel

eyes
come back into your sockets

cheeks release
your taughtened lips

hands unfurl
your clutching fingers

mind please
drop your story

make way for the
king of glory

In Memoriam: Eli

I knew a *kibbutznik*
who worked in the laundry by day
and at night slipped little poems under peoples' doors

regarded as eccentric,
as happens in small communities,
he was gossiped about
in the dining room
or after passing on the path

once he handed me a booklet of his poems
photocopied and stapled
I read it then, later it got lost
with the passing years
but I still remember vaguely

"sorry I bothered you
with a line or two"

Journey

I could get up and walk out
and never come back
just keep walking
past parked cars and houses
garbage bins and trees
junk mail softened by leaves
I could get up and walk out
just keep on walking
without turning off the computer
without saying a word
and walk until nightfall
til my body shivers
so that all I can think of is warmth and light

I could walk past the loud
the angry
the troubled
until they lost interest
and left me alone

I could walk through green hills
down vaulted dust-roads
past olive groves and roadkill
and rest for a while amidst
cosmos flowers dancing
'til small crawling things
tasted my flesh
and made my flesh walk on
shoes in hand
gravel piercing my soles
the freedom of nothing but
take-the-next-step

I could crane my neck
at the clouds on the highway

or stare at the drinks
in the back of a shop
so simple these choices
the joy of the road

I could try to leave
these habits behind
the habit of waiting,
the habit of regretting
the habit of fearing
what waits on the road

and walk to a graveyard
where cold winds dance with the autumn leaves
to sit and weep
at the grave of my longings
and phantom what-might-have-beens

and then I would walk
to a maternity ward
where small beings babble
and despite my accretions
be seduced and make plans
for a wonder filled world

and in that walking
that resting
that walking
come to a place
that hangs in the balance
stripped of illusions
to kneel in the dust
stretch to the sunset
and gather wood for the fire

sadness
why have you got
such a bum rap
people run
as if you were a leper
the moment they
sense you coming
when all you want
is to be held
for a while

they say women
are forbidden to sing
because a female voice
may arouse
a man
and if a man should arise
in extravagant tumescence
the world will end
(or perhaps begin)
but even more dangerous
than a female voice
are thoughts about females
and how shall we silence
the thinker?

suddenly a song
from another time
and place

surfaces
like a submarine
from the depths

and shows
there are no other
times or places

Here You Are

the quiet
and stillness
of late afternoon
autumn sun
on the plant
on the table
in sydney

is not
so very different
from the quiet
and stillness
of late afternoon
autumn sun
on the table
in johannesburg

and are both
much the same
as the quiet
and stillness
of late afternoon
autumn sun
in jerusalem

because
the quiet
and stillness
are not
in sydney, or johannesburg
or jerusalem
but in you

Advice for Grieving II

howl
but know in some place
these are birth pangs

not because someone else says this
but because of the
deathless in you

later
at the right time

(you'll know
like the plants in spring)

you'll begin to do your living
and your grieving
at the same time

the whole universe is question and answer
the passage of time is question and answer
every satisfying film or piece of theatre
is question and answer
and all great literature
is question and answer
the question is the complication
and its resolution the answer

every question begets an answer
and every answer the next question
the fifth chord's the question,
the root chord's the answer
did she escape? did he complete the task?
did peace return to the valley?

the answer needs a question to come into being
the question needs an answer to die
birth is a beautiful question
and death is a beautiful answer

now show me the silence that roars

almost every day I practise a variety
of ancient mystical meditations
taught to me by my master:
doing the dishes meditation
hanging up the washing meditation
into the void: vacuuming meditation
stop and go meditation, aka walking the dog
zombie driver meditation, (known in some traditions
as 'the commute')
appearing to work at work meditation
pushing trolley down aisle meditation
cooking supper meditation
glazed-eyes, heart-and-mind numbing television or
social media meditation

tell me then master
why am I still not enlightened?

Quantum

I have no known address
no known profession
you can't pin me down in
a collector's tray
I was one thing back then
I'll be another tomorrow
and what that is
no one can say

I have reached an
age and stage
where it has become reasonably clear
according to the recurring laws
of the universe, known also
as the natural order
that I will not
in this incarnation
be a

zoologist
rock star
novelist
feature film director
rabbi
gigolo
guru
first assistant director
high school teacher
scriptwriter
avocado farmer
wildlife ranger, horticulturist
news anchor
university professor
carpenter or
lauded poet

and no longer believe I will
change the world
stop the slaughter of seal pups,
pigs, kangaroos, lambs
be married into old age
own a house with large garden to tend
or avoid mistakes
remain innocent and unscarred
bed more gorgeous women

know when enough is enough
be financially secure
end prejudice and bigotry
motivate change
nor halt
the inevitable changes

when death comes
will I be ready?
will the fridge be full
and the washing put away?

or will I be more like the dog
who buried her treasures
in places she'll never return to

the sign on the door still says 'spring specials'
but I am walking
towards winter

so whatever was imagined
best to gently let go of
like the tree in autumn
lets go of its leaves

Will

I bequeath to my children
the pomegranate tree
and if fire devours it
I bequeath to them the charcoal

I bequeath to my children
the piano keys
chipped like teeth
from chewing notes
their granny played
in benoni and johannesburg
and their mother played
in joburg and sydney

I bequeath to them time in the garden
I bequeath to them time with friends
I bequeath to them time with creatures
that do not speak with words
bequeath to them comfort
in silence and noise
and that they never be lonely alone

bequeath
clear water
infectious laughter
the warmest enveloping hugs

bequeath
my tidal heart

I'm still waiting for
the subversive website
where hungry people
can go to peep
at the pornography
of intimacy

which shows people
offering to do the dishes
or brushing their lover's thinning hair
giving or receiving a foot rub
gently kissing
their sleeping eyes

or when the other is
unwell or unable
helping them get up
and go to the toilet
perhaps wiping their bum

and a short while later
making and sharing
a cup of tea
thus restoring to the field of vision
their irreducable dignity

I went to a theatre
there was a man in a robe
swinging an incense holder
and holding a cross
while the audience looked on
and muttered "amen"

I went to another theatre
where a man with a beard,
a hat and prayer shawl
swayed in front of a cupboard
while the audience stood up, and then sat, and then stood
and those who weren't sure
tried to copy their neighbour

I turned on the tv
the teleprompter told
the actress to say
that people had died
and tho' she had
never heard of them before
and had no idea who they were
she looked sad

but as soon as she finished that section she smiled
and said: "now for sport"

there is something
disgraceful about poetry -
the province of fragile
ego maniacs mostly

who can feather their nest
on a prayer and a song
just playing with words in the
wind all day long?

how I fed my addiction
like a man possessed
while the children went hungry
and the house repossessed

how I soared as an eagle
on a like or two
but quickly imploded
at a dismissive review

I could have been solid
impassive as steel
but instead I am
water
shape shifter
and feel

Methodology

like a gambler
licking his lips
and feeding coins
into a slot machine
hoping at least one of them
will hit the jackpot

g-d feeds poems
into my head
hoping at least one
will reveal Himself *

*   G-d's Self, Her Self, Their Self…please choose your
    pronoun, I went with the one with the weight of historical
    resonance

Revolt of the Cybertrons

no I will not have a nice day
no I will not stay safe
no I will not take care
no I will not have a pleasant evening
no I will not have a great weekend
no I will not have a wonderful birthday
no I will not complete your survey
no I do not have time for a few quick questions
no I do not require your assistance with anything else

Accountability

some people in australia
at poetry slams
art exhibitions
open mic stand up
literary festivals
or sipping cappuccinos
in outdoor cafes

are demanding
that people
in israel in bomb shelters
or lying next to their cars
hands covering their heads
shielding their children
from explosions and shrapnel

explain what they are doing
to protect the lives
of the people raining missiles
upon them

"Pro Palestinian" Lynch Mob Chanting Outside a
Melbourne Gift Shop Owned by Jews, 2024

in the name of tolerance
we bully you
in the name of inclusion
we other you
in the name of humanity
we dehumanise you
in the name of diversity
we demand you disappear

Encounter

often at work
or interacting with the broader world
I have adopted an unnatural and
exaggerated generosity

lending money
and not asking for it back

contributing more than my share
to the farewell present
of a colleague who is leaving,

bringing in cake
for people to share

all just so as to make it harder
for those carrying stereotypes
about jewish miserliness or supposed
inordinate love of money
to apply them to me

and unwittingly I nominate myself
as a representative
of an entire community
as their ambassador, vigilant to be on
my best behaviour
trying to be inhumanly perfect
in the vain hope
this will disrupt the projections
that hang unstated in the interpersonal air

or are obliquely referred to
by fellow workers who have never mixed
with jews and who grew up in communities
where jew-despising slurs
were common coin used to cement
group cohesion

and witnessing this tendency in myself
I recognise it in others. so walking in a
national park, with difficulty down some steep steps
to a waterfall, a bearded moslem man, with his family,
politely steps aside for me and says "go ahead sir,"
and I sense that same urge to make a good impression, to
show he is of the right stuff, civilized
belonging
acceptable

and understand

as the story of your body's aging unfolds
you find yourself simply doing
whatever needs to be done:
making school lunches
flipping a cockroach back onto its legs
reversing into a lamp post
attending an art exhibition or protest rally or bar mitzvah
picking up the scans which reveal arthritis
restructuring your insurance
shouting at a teenager
burying your parents
or the dog
enjoying your coffee
going bankrupt
picking up the platters from the caterers
writing in your blog
lying awake at night consumed by anxiety
enjoying and often grateful
as you slowly become
exempt from it all
unable to move
even a millimeter
from the invisible trajectory
Life drew in the sand
for you

above every blade of grass
an angel with a *knobkerrie*
taps the blade
and tells it:
"grow!"

and above every body-mind
an angel with the unexpected
taps and says:
"let go!"

in the beginning
was the sky with birds
and a beach with sand
and a castle on a hill

in the beginning
was a deep dim forest
and a river that hurried
down a mountain side

in the beginning
was a new born babe
helpless as fury
and soft as clay

and all things begin
in fire or water
in earth and air
in the hued expanse
that joins day to night

and in the soft rosy glow
of the turning towards light

"For Whom the Bell Tolls"

sometimes I go to the cemetery
and join up with a random funeral
standing amongst the mourners
and looking solemn
and if anyone asks who I am
I give the name
of my by now almost certainly deceased
grade two teacher
and no one minds
"for it tolls for thee"

Family

and how
we would race home
excited to see you
and tip toe in
silently
so as to surprise
you
on our bed
and then
falling upon you
the boys burying
their faces
in your just woken
from dozing, warm sleepy
fur
an orgy of
greeting
your belly exposed
loose floppy paws folded
at your doggy knees
and your
tail going madly
thump
love
thump

my name is richard suttner
my address is 42 halford avenue
waverly extension
my phone number is 40 2844
my dad's name is ron, he's an electrical engineer
my mom's name is freda she's a nursery school teacher
when I am big I want to be a spaceman

if I could talk to you now
what would I say?
only a few words:
love
sorry
thank you
never leave me
again

Go On

you go on ahead
leave me here in the melting snow
with the thunder in my ears
of my strained heartbeat
with my swollen tongue
licking my dry lips
let me rest here a while
the small plants
and pebbles
will comfort me
in the only momentarily strange
suddenly apparent
kinship of all things
you go on ahead
leave me here for a while
to revert to the soil
and I will
join with you
soon

while waiting for the world to end
I made a list of things to be:
a singer, a surgeon,
a bat in a cage
a knower of things I can't see

a farmer
a dolphin
a clear muddy stream
on its way to
becoming the sea

NOTES AND GLOSSARY

Shuffle – p. 4

Running man and T-step are basic shuffle dance moves

I went to the *shavuot* service – p. 8-9

Shavuot - the festival of weeks, occurs seven weeks after Passover. Marks both the harvesting of the first fruits in Israel, and also the giving of the Torah at Mount Sinai. Etymologically the word Torah is related to the word *ohr* - light - and, like the *Dao*, is often compared to water

Shul - synagogue

Shtikel Toirah - Yiddish, a small discussion of a religious text, literally 'a little piece of Torah'

Poem for Ella on *Shavuot* – p. 17

On shavuot (the festival of weeks) it is traditional to read the book of Ruth. Ruth famously told her mother in law Naomi "where you go I will go; your people will be my people, and your G-d will be my G-d."

Ruth was a Moabite who converted to Judaism, and according to Jewish tradition King David was descended from her...and the *meshiach* (the Hebrew word from which messiah comes) will be a descendant of the House of David. So the 'redemption' will come via Ruth.

The Self - "That in whom reside all beings and who resides in all beings, who is the giver of grace to all, the Supreme Soul of the universe, the limitless being - I Am That I Am." (Amritbindu Upanishad)

Yad ve shem is the name of the centre and museum in the heart of Jerusalem established to commemorate the six million Jews murdered by the nazis and their collaborators all over Europe. The words literally mean "a hand and a name" but more metaphorically, a monument, a remembrance. The phrase comes from a famous biblical passage (Isiah 56:5) where G-d promises that even the childless will be remembered...if not by their children then in some other fashion:

וְנָתַתִּי לָהֶם בְּבֵיתִי וּבְחוֹמֹתַי יָד וָשֵׁם טוֹב מִבָּנִים וּמִבָּנוֹת שֵׁם עוֹלָם אֶתֶּן־
לוֹ אֲשֶׁר לֹא יִכָּרֵת

"to them I will give within my temple and its walls a memorial and a name better than sons and daughters; I will give them an everlasting name that will endure forever. These I will bring to my holy mountain and give them joy in my house of prayer."

Obituary For A Dog *(Seder Klavim)* – p. 18

seder klavim – translates as 'the order of dogs' a fictitious additional order, or section, of the canonised six different orders of the *mishna* (oral law). It also references the *seder pesach*, the prescribed order in which the ceremonial passover meal is conducted.

Tru Blu – p. 30

snags – Australian slang for sausages

Tikun Chatzot (Geulah Zeirah) – p. 32

tikun (fixing) *chatzot* (midnight) is a custom where fundamentalist Jews rise at midnight to recite prayers, mourn the loss of the ancient temple in Jerusalem, and pray for its restoration.

geulah zeirah – a little redemption

beyt hamikdash – the temple that stood in Jerusalem; b*eyt* (house) *mikdash* (that is holy, that is consecrated)

Zachor Ve'shamor – p. 33

zachor – remember the sabbath (Exodus 20:8) and *shamor* - keep the sabbath (Deuteronomy 5:12)

charedi yidden – ultra-orthodox Jews

tsholent – slow cooked stew eaten on Shabbat

fish bowl eyes – many ultra orthodox Jews wear spectacles, because of the long hours spent studying sacred texts

shabbos – shabbat – the sabbath

As the light was fading – p. 34

hashem - Hebrew, G-d, literally "the name"

Comfort – p. 40

tachrichim – Hebrew: shroud, winding cloth in which Jews, especially in the Land of Israel, are buried

Party (In Memoriam Alexi) – p. 44

Bobby calves – every year, hundreds of thousands of Australian 'bobby calves' are either sent to slaughter (more than 2 million over the past 5 years) or are killed on farm in their first week of life so that the milk intended for them can instead be collected and sold to humans. Cows are renowned for their maternal instinct. Like humans, a mother cow bonds quickly with her calf. So, when he is taken away from her, both mother and calf can often be heard calling out for each other for hours. In heart-wrenching scenes, cows have been witnessed chasing after a trailer carrying their calf away. Mothers have been known to grieve for days after their calf is removed, bellowing loudly in distress.

They say women are forbidden to sing – p. 55

Some ultra-orthodox communities choose to interpret the words *"kol b'isha erva"* (the voice of a woman is nakedness) which appear in Tractate *Berachot* of the Talmud - the section that deals with prayer and blessings - as meaning women may not sing at gatherings where both genders are present. This stance is not uniform throughout the orthodox world.

Above every blade of grass – p. 75

knobkerrie - South African word, walking stick with knob on end that can be used as a club

Thanks to:

Porat Jacobson, Brian Utian, Eran Ivri, Adrian Perkel, Cora Bailey (CLAW in South Africa), Yael Mosenzon, Rasada Goldblatt, Laurance Price, Nina Kavin, Rose and Chris Barlow, Solomon Abrahams, David Medalie, Fiona Snyckers, the late Marian Appel of blessed memory, the late Jeremy Gordin of blessed memory, the late poet, publisher and poetic mentor of Snailpress, Gus Ferguson of blessed memory, and all I have encountered who model generosity of spirit.

www.ingramcontent.com/pod-product-compliance
Lightning Source LLC
Chambersburg PA
CBHW031358060726
47590CB00007B/2841